TRUCKS, TRAINS AND BIG MACHINES!

TRANSPORTATION BOOKS FOR KIDS
CHILDREN'S TRANSPORTATION BOOKS

D1535951

BABY PROFESSOR
EDUCATION KIDS

CHARLIE

Speedy Publishing LLC

40 E. Main St. #1156

Newark, DE 19711

www.speedypublishing.com

Copyright 2017

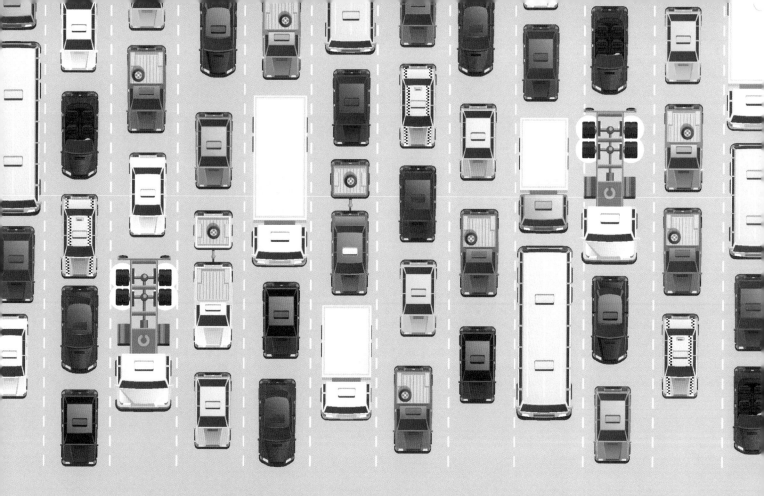

In this book, we're going to talk about trucks, trains, and other big transportation and work machines. So, let's get right to it!

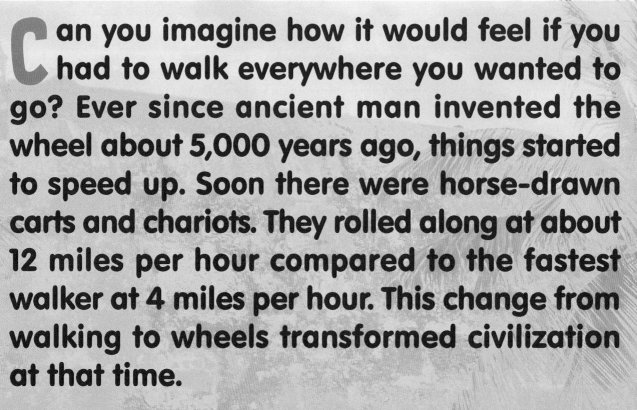

Can you imagine how it would feel if you had to walk everywhere you wanted to go? Ever since ancient man invented the wheel about 5,000 years ago, things started to speed up. Soon there were horse-drawn carts and chariots. They rolled along at about 12 miles per hour compared to the fastest walker at 4 miles per hour. This change from walking to wheels transformed civilization at that time.

HORSE DRAWN CARRIAGES

In the late 1800s, inventors started to experiment with steam and gasoline engines and these new inventions caused a giant leap forward for transportation around the world. Soon there were trucks, trains, tractors, and fire engines, powered by steam or gasoline. All these transportation inventions helped people to get from place to place, helped them move heavy goods or livestock from one destination to another, and helped them get work done.

STEAM ENGINE TRAIN

There are lots of different types of trucks that you might see traveling on the road every day. Trucks are classified by the amount of weight they can carry. Most trucks carry a few people and they can also carry cargo. The bigger types of trucks can carry lots of people, supplies, or livestock. Some of the biggest types of trucks help do construction work.

BIG TRUCK

CLASS 1

These trucks carry 6,000 pounds or less. Small minivans are in this category and so are full-size pickups and small vans used for delivering lightweight goods like flowers.

CLASS 2

This type of truck can carry from 6,001 to 10,000 pounds of weight. Step vans that deliver packages are class 2 trucks. Large pickup trucks that farmers use to haul supplies fall in this category also.

CLASS 3

This type of truck has a cab and a large rectangular back section for hauling goods from 10,001 to 14,000 pounds. This class also has walk-in type trucks that deliver supplies.

CLASS 4

These trucks can carry from 14,001 to 16,000 pounds of weight. Larger walk-in trucks, like United Parcel Service trucks, local delivery trucks, and conventional vans fall in this category.

This type of truck can haul from 16,001 to 19,500 pounds of weight. Larger local delivery and walk-in trucks fit in this category. Also, a special type of truck called a bucket truck that is used to lift workers and supplies up to cut trees, to repair signs and traffic signals, and to fix power lines is also in the Class 5 category.

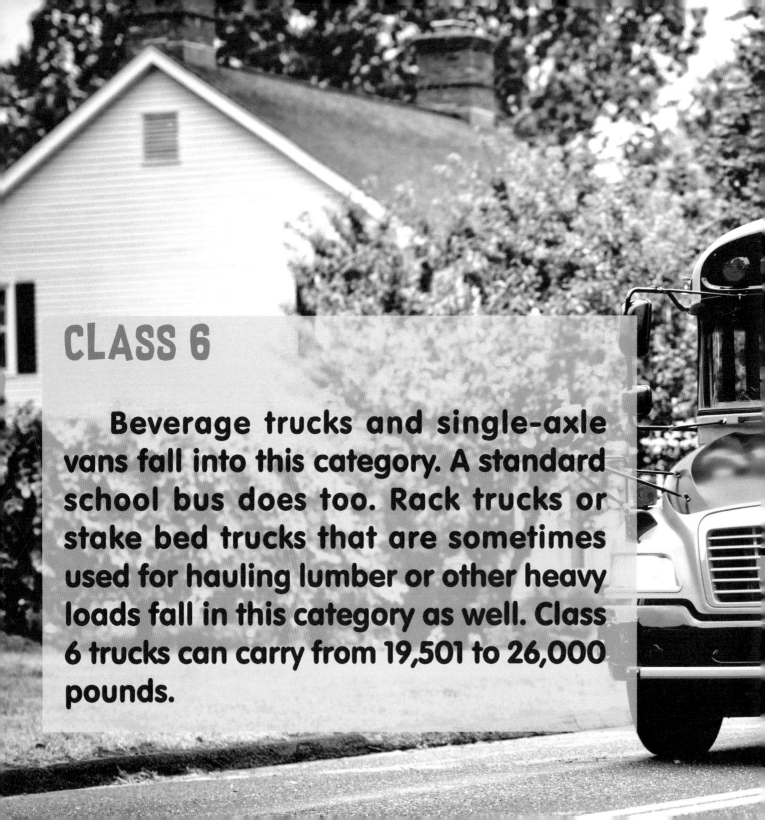

CLASS 6

Beverage trucks and single-axle vans fall into this category. A standard school bus does too. Rack trucks or stake bed trucks that are sometimes used for hauling lumber or other heavy loads fall in this category as well. Class 6 trucks can carry from 19,501 to 26,000 pounds.

CLASS 7

Garbage trucks and recycling trucks fall into Class 7 and can haul 26,001 to 33,000 pounds of garbage. Furniture trucks or moving trucks fall into this category too. A city transit bus as well as a truck that can haul a flatbed are also Class 7 trucks.

CLASS 8

Class 8 trucks include dump trucks and cement trucks that are used on construction sites. This class also includes heavy conventional trucks and sleeper trucks for long hauls across the country. They can haul a massive weight that's 33,001 pounds or heavier!

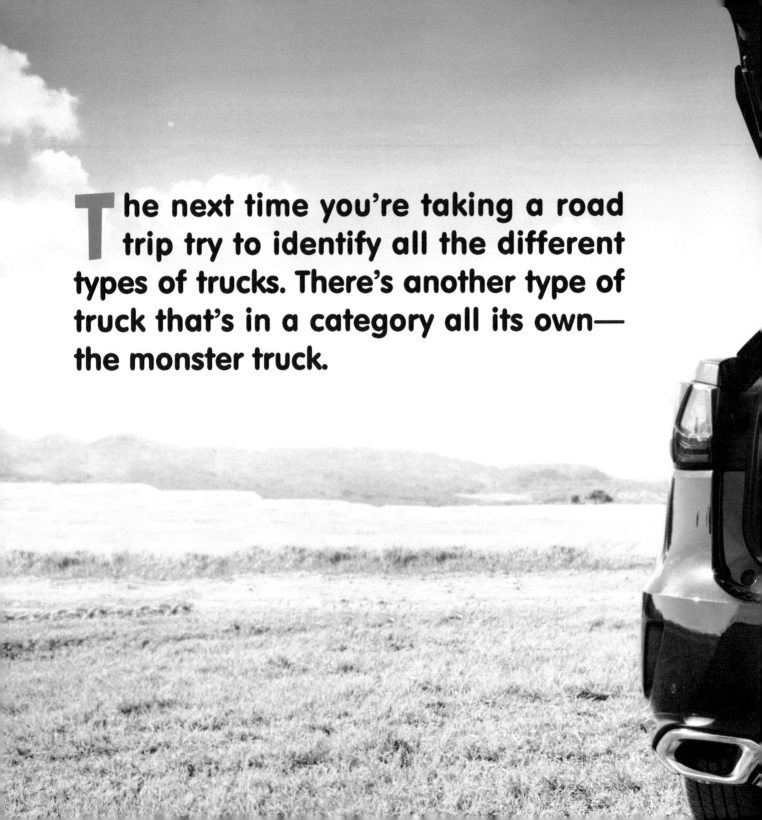

The next time you're taking a road trip try to identify all the different types of trucks. There's another type of truck that's in a category all its own— the monster truck.

ob Chandler built the very first monster truck in 1979. It was named Bigfoot. Since then, these huge trucks with the monster-sized wheels have been entertaining huge crowds by racing over dirt roads, doing stunts, jumping off ramps, and crushing cars.

A monster truck starts out as a regular standard-sized pickup truck. The body is kept, but then a large steel frame and enormous tires are added. These tires are 5 feet 7 inches tall. The driver is held in with a racing harness as he maneuvers the monster truck to do its amazing stunts.

MONSTER TRUCK

eginning in the 1500s, people in Europe filled wagons with coal and mineral ore to get it out of mines. People and horses pulled the heavy wagons on rails and it was backbreaking work for man and beast. Travel by railway was faster than travel on roads, since the wagons wouldn't hit bumps and could hold heavier loads. About 300 years later, a mechanical "beast" was created that could do this heavy work so people and horses didn't have to do it anymore. It was the steam locomotive.

Richard Trevithick built the first working steam locomotive in 1804. It pulled five cars filled with 10 tons of iron as well as 70 workers. Unfortunately, it was so heavy it broke its rails after just three trips. However, Trevithick didn't give up. In 1808, he built another locomotive that pulled a four-wheeled car. A few brave passengers got on and went around a circular track in the middle of London.

STEPHENSON'S "ROCKET"

In 1829, a contest was held to select the best design for a locomotive. Robert Stephenson won the contest with his steam locomotive called the Rocket. It traveled at a top speed of 29 miles per hour. The Rocket was used to pull railway cars on the first train route from Liverpool to Manchester in the United Kingdom.

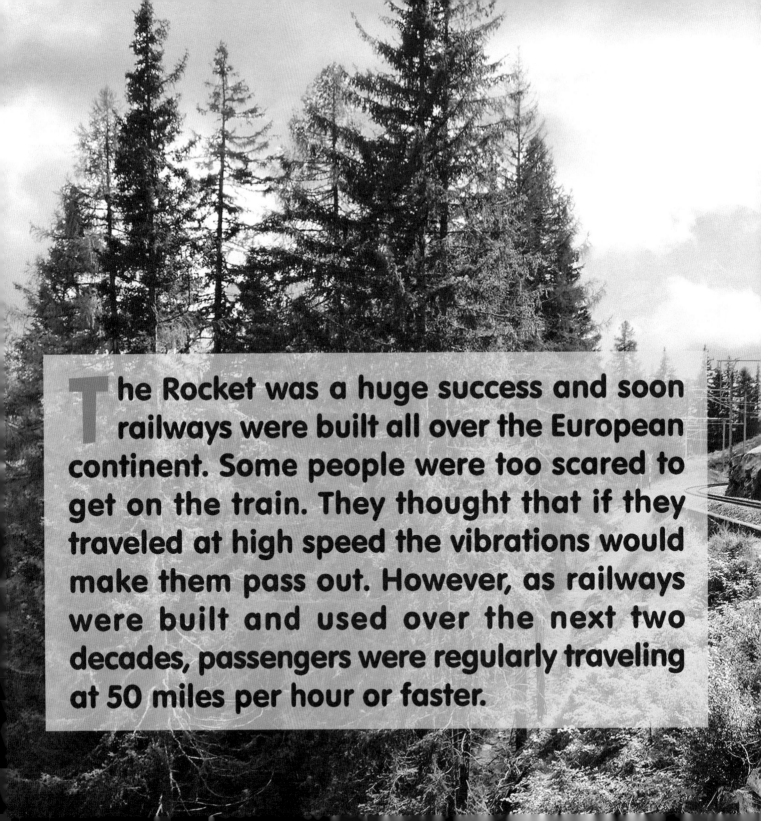

The Rocket was a huge success and soon railways were built all over the European continent. Some people were too scared to get on the train. They thought that if they traveled at high speed the vibrations would make them pass out. However, as railways were built and used over the next two decades, passengers were regularly traveling at 50 miles per hour or faster.

Soon train tracks were being built in the United States. The railroad in the US was built from 1863 through 1869 by the Central Pacific and Union Pacific railway companies. On May 10, 1869, the final link between the eastern and western railroads was completed to create the first United States Transcontinental Railroad. Now goods and people could be transported from east to west and back by steam trains. In 1871, New York City opened its famous Grand Central Station. Today, more than 700,000 people pass through the station every day.

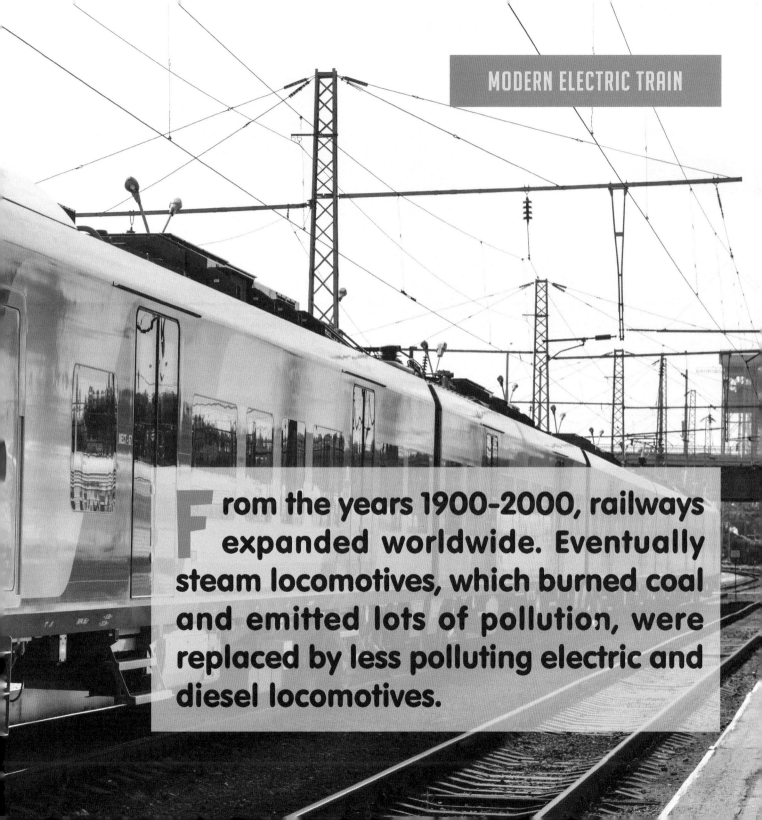

MODERN ELECTRIC TRAIN

From the years 1900-2000, railways expanded worldwide. Eventually steam locomotives, which burned coal and emitted lots of pollution, were replaced by less polluting electric and diesel locomotives.

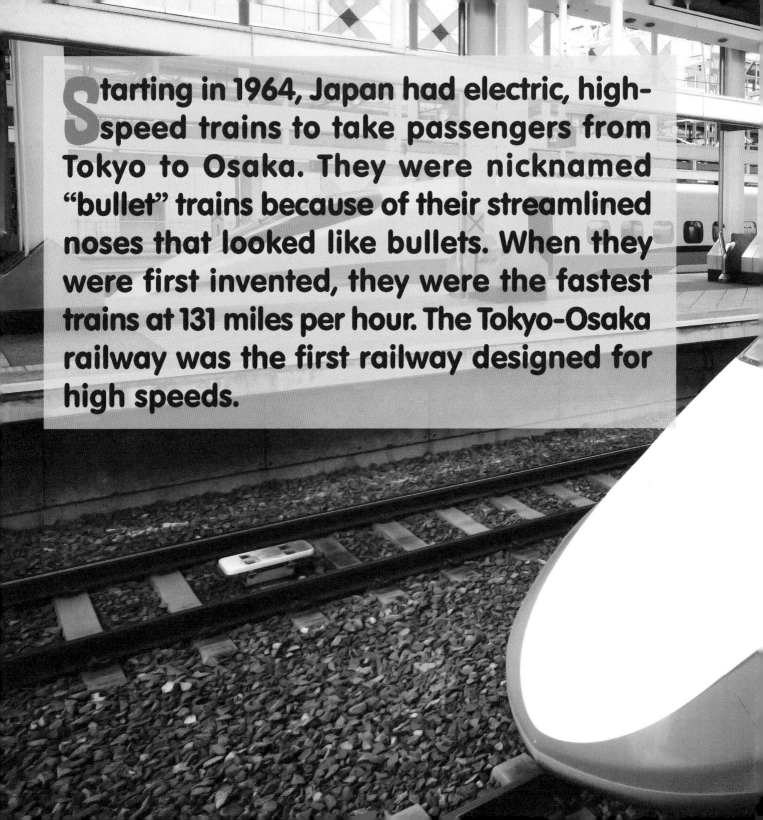

Starting in 1964, Japan had electric, high-speed trains to take passengers from Tokyo to Osaka. They were nicknamed "bullet" trains because of their streamlined noses that looked like bullets. When they were first invented, they were the fastest trains at 131 miles per hour. The Tokyo-Osaka railway was the first railway designed for high speeds.

HIGH SPEED BULLET TRAIN

n 2003, Japan started to use an experimental maglev train, which set a new record for speed at 361 miles per hour. Maglev means magnetic levitation. These trains are supported by electromagnetic attraction or repulsion on their tracks. They actually float about an inch above their tracks as they run!

HIGH-SPEED COMMUTER TRAIN

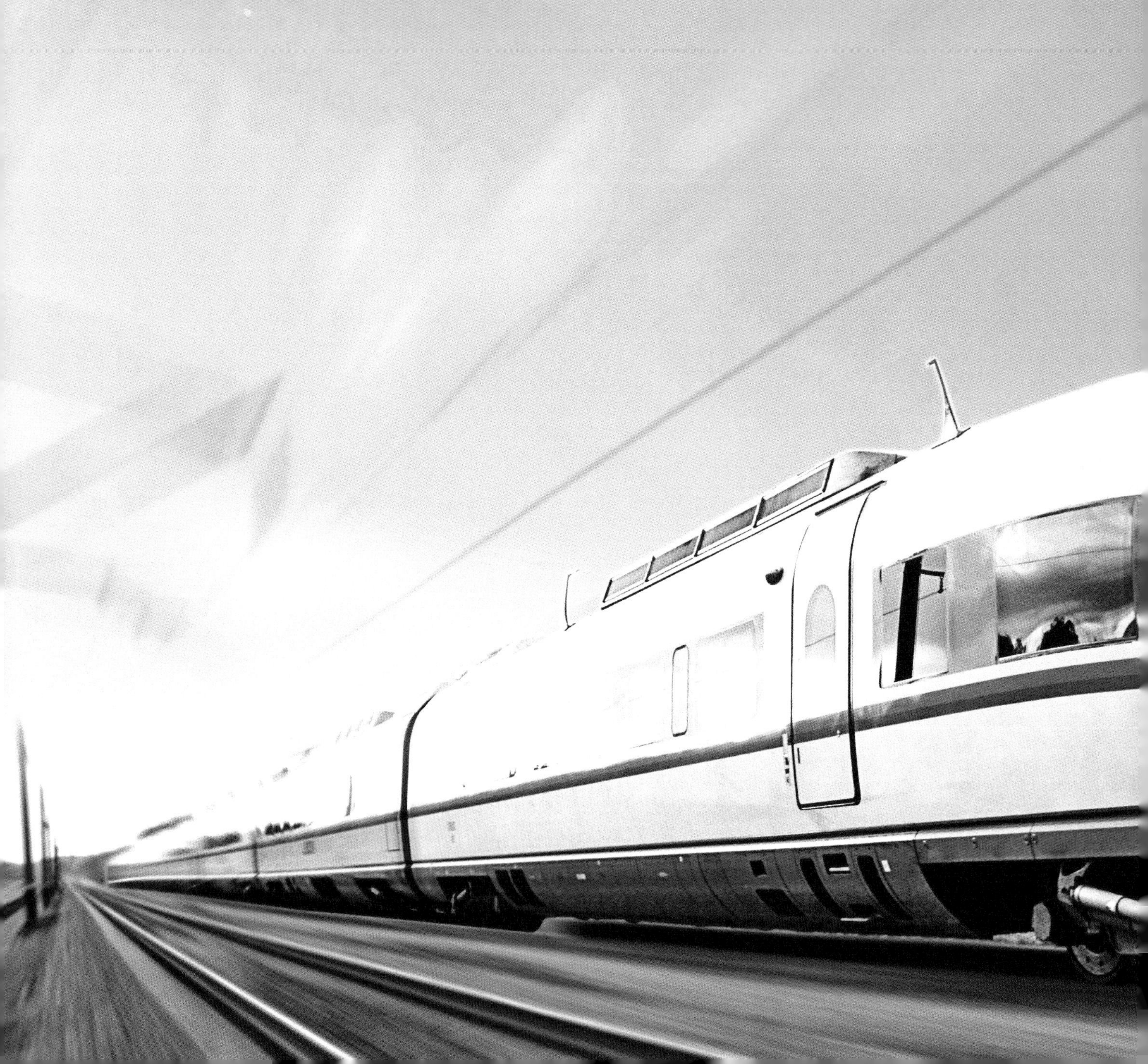

Today, high-speed trains are used worldwide. In France, the TGV runs at 200 to 300 miles per hour. That's twice the speed of a racecar! In the US, high-speed commuter trains carry business passengers between the major cities on the East Coast.

TRACTOR WITH A TANK FOR TRANSPORTING GRAIN

TRACTORS

Tractors help us produce our food. They also help workers maintain our roads and parks. When they were first designed, they were simple machines on wheels of steel, but today they are complicated machines that do specialized work.

The earliest tractors were first put into use around 1900. They were used to pull heavy farm machines. They were effective, but they moved very slowly. If you are waiting for a tractor to move along on a highway, it can be frustrating.

Most vehicles started with steam-powered engines and tractors were no exception. Eventually, more powerful and cleaner-running diesel and gas engines became standard.

here are three types of fire trucks that might show up to help put out a fire. In addition to the equipment they hold, fire trucks can carry up to eight firefighters. They sit in the truck's cab on the way to the fire.

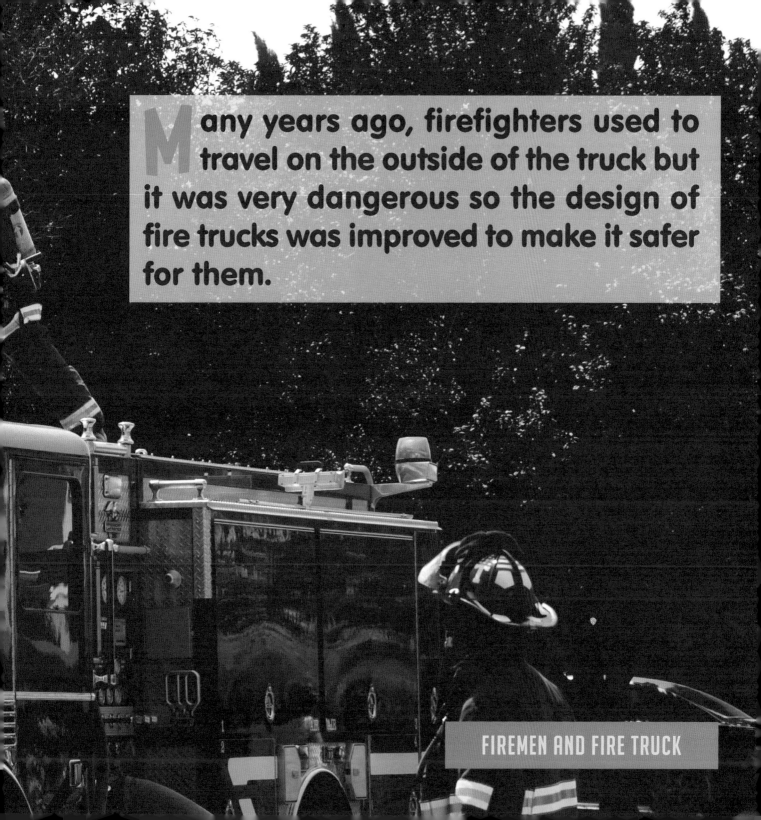

Many years ago, firefighters used to travel on the outside of the truck but it was very dangerous so the design of fire trucks was improved to make it safer for them.

FIREMEN AND FIRE TRUCK

TANKER TRUCKS

Most average tanker trucks carry about 1,000 gallons of water to help put out fires. There are also huge tanker trucks that carry up to 5,000 gallons of water. These larger tanker trucks are used in areas where there are no fire hydrants.

FIRE DEPARTMENT PUMPER RESCUE TRUCK

PUMPER TRUCKS

Pumper Trucks are 30 feet in length and they hold some water. However, they are designed to pump water out from a water source like a fire hydrant, lake, or swimming pool. Some trucks are combinations of pumpers and tankers.

LADDER TRUCKS

Ladder Trucks are longer than the other two types of fire trucks. They are usually about 40 to 50 feet in length and they have long, telescopic ladders so that firefighters can climb up to the tops of office or apartment buildings.

Awesome! Now you know more about trucks, trains, and other big machines. You can find more Transportation books from Baby Professor by searching the website of your favorite book retailer.

Visit

BABY PROFESSOR
EDUCATION KIDS

www.BabyProfessorBooks.com
to download Free Baby Professor eBooks
and view our catalog of new and exciting
Children's Books

Made in the USA
Columbia, SC
17 April 2018